NONE
DARE
CALL
IT
TREASON!
BOOK 16

Security Risks
In The
House and Senate

Robert W. Pelton
$4.95

"*Treason doth never prosper,*

"*What's the reason?*

"*Why if it prosper,*

"*None dare call it treason.*"

John Harrington

Printed in America
On Recycled Paper
In
Charleston, South Carolina

Published in America
By
The Freedom & Liberty
Foundation Press
Knoxville, Tennessee

Dedicated
To

The greatest, most generous, most benevolent and most powerful nation on the face of the earth – and the only country in the history of the world to have been founded on Biblical principles.

A nation can survive its fools, and even the ambitious. But it cannot survive treason from within.

An enemy at the gates is less formidable, for he is known and he carries his banners openly.

The traitor moves among those within the gates freely, his sly whispers rustling through the galleys, heard in the very hall of government itself.

For the traitor appears not traitor. He speaks in the accent familiar to his victims, and he wears their face and their garments, and he appeals to the baseness that lies deep in the hearts of all men.

He rots the soul of a nation - he works secretly and unknown in the night to undermine the pillars of a city - he infects the body politic so that it can no longer resist.

A murderer is less to be feared.

Cicero, 42 B.C.

CONTENTS

Forward

Independence Hall Where the Declaration of Independence Was Signed.

Our glorious Declaration of Independence is a timeless divinely inspired masterpiece given to mankind through the anointed pen of Thomas Jefferson. The grand and unmatched United States Constitution is indisputably the product of Providential guidance and wisdom and certainly not a document which evokes whimsical interpretations with the changing political climates.

All Americans have a moral obligation to stand up and be counted in these trying times!

Abraham Lincoln boldly declared: *"To sin by silence when they should protest, makes cowards of men."*

William Lloyd Garrison capsulized it best: *"As a free man who is determined to remain free -- I do not wish to think or speak, or write with moderation. "Tell a man whose house is on fire to give a moderate alarm; tell him to moderately rescue his wife from the hands of a ravisher; tell the mother to gradually extricate her babe from the fire into which it has fallen -- but urge me not to use moderation in a course like the present."*

Senator Barry Goldwater, 1964 Presidential candidate was castigated and verbally crucified by the media.

14

He simply stated this simple truism: *"Extremism in the pursuit of Liberty is no vice."*

This good and moral man of character soundly rocked the boat of the propagandists. He was as a result soundly defeated in the election.

The alarmed media wolves panicked the voters with their jeers and sneers and insane howls about this man's lack of *"moderation!"*

It can honestly be said that through the Providential genius of our Founding Fathers, the remaining remnants of the original American Constitutional Republic still provides more freedom, opportunity and abundance for mankind than is found in any other nation in the world.

This is true despite decade after decade of unabated treason and treachery promulgated by innumerable traitorous individuals found buried in the twiddle dee – twiddle dum administrations of both the Democrats and the Republicans.

An informed and active, not a media brainwashed electorate, is the only antidote to further prostitution of, and the ultimate destruction of, what Benjamin Franklin called our Republic.

Preface

"Treason against the United States shall consist only in levying war against them, or in adhering to their enemies, giving them aid and comfort."

U.S. Constitution. Article 111, Section 3

What is your treason I.Q.?

If you can answer the following questions, it's high.

If you miss one or more, you should read the *None Dare Call It Treason* series!

Who was behind allowing Red Chinese soldiers take airborne training at Fort Benning, Georgia?

Is this not treason?

Why was South Vietnam, South Africa, Rhodesia and numerous other American friends deliberately betrayed to the forces of evil?

Is this not treason?

Why was our friend Chiang Kai Shek not so gently coerced into a Communist dictatorship by highly placed subversives in the State Department?

Is this not treason?

Why was Cuba treasonously delivered into the clutches of Communist revolutionary Fidel Castro?

Is this not treason?

Why have untold millions of dollars consistently been used to prop up faltering Red dictatorships and to assist Communist terrorists in overthrowing non-Communist governments?

Is this not treason?

What American company sold nuclear reactors to Communist Occupied Romania?

Is this not treason?

Name the company that provided Communist Hungary with a factory designed to make 1.5 million light bulbs daily?

Is this not treason?

What well known oil company invested $1 billion for oil exploration in Communist Occupied Angola?

Is this not treason?

Can you name the American company who treasonously built and equipped a $10 million electronics plant near Warsaw for the Polish slave labor tyranny?

Is this not treason?

These are questions to which every American should rightfully have an honest answer.

Unfortunately most do not!

Tragedy was carefully orchestrated by traitors in our Government and the media with regard to Cuba, Vietnam, Laos, Cambodia, Rhodesia, China, El Salvador, Nicaragua and many other countries.   Anastasio   Somoza was the former President of free Nicaragua.

He offered this startling insight in his 1980 book, Nicaragua Betrayed: *"I have factual evidence that the betrayal of Nicaragua was not perpetrated out of ignorance, but rather by design."*

Somoza was soon after assassinated!

Is this not treason?

John Lehman, Secretary of the Navy, made this shocking statement on May 25 to the 1983 Annapolis graduating class: *"Within weeks many of you will be looking across just hundreds of feet of water at some of the most modern technology ever invented in America.*

"Unfortunately, it is on Soviet ships."

Is this not treason?

Earl E.T. Smith was the American Ambassador to Cuba when it was similarly delivered to the Communists.

He makes this concise comment on July 14, 1986: *"Nicaragua is Cuba all over again."*

Can you name the company that paid the Communist dictatorship in Angola over $600 million annually in taxes and oil royalties.

This money bought new Soviet jets, tanks and helicopter gunships.

And it paid Castro for supplying 35,000 imported Cuban mercenaries who keep the Angolan people enslaved.

Is this not treason?

Stressed retired Brigadier General Andrew J. Gatsis on August 11, 1986: *"Though aware of the Communist goal of world domination, the average U.S. Citizen refuses to believe that the real threat comes from governmental officials and their non-governmental confederates who secretly espouse the same objectives as the openly avowed Communists."*

Anthony Sutton stated in his 1986 book *The Best Enemy Money Can Buy: "We now have the formidable task of bringing these gentlemen to the bar of justice to publicly answer for their private and*

concealed actions."

The *None Dare Call It Treason* series certainly won't win accolades from the United Nations or the State Department!

Nor will Harvard feel compelled to bestow an honorary degree upon the author!

Harvard Law School was the spawning ground for an incredible number of Red agents. Included were members of the first Soviet spy ring ever to be exposed in our government.

Reed Irvine aptly commented in July of 1986: *"Indeed, it has long been a joke among refugees from Eastern Europe that there are more Marxists at Harvard than there are in the Soviet Union, or Poland, or whatever Communist country the refugee called home."*

The Honorable Ezra Taft Benson said: *"The truth must be told even at the risk of*

destroying, in large measure, the influence of
men who are widely respected and loved by
the American people.

"The stakes are high. Freedom and survival is the issue."

Treason is still a most serious federal offense.

The *None Dare Call It Treason* series examines the reasons for and the Americans behind the fall of freedom and the rise of tyranny throughout the world!

Has anything really changed?
You Decide!

Treason

Whoever, owing allegiance to the United States, levies war against them or adheres to their enemies, giving them aid and comfort within the United States or elsewhere, is guilty of treason and shall suffer death, or be imprisoned not less than five years and fined not less than $10,000; and shall be incapable of holding any office under the United states.

U.S. Code, Title 18, Section 2381

Whoever, owing allegiance to the United States and having knowledge of the commission of any treason against them, conceals and does not, as soon as may be, disclose and make known the same to the President or to some judge of the United States, or to the Governor or to some judge or justice of a particular state, is guilty of misprision of treason, and shall be fined not more than $1000 or imprisoned not more than 7 years or both.

U.S. Code, Title 18, Section 2382

Security Risks

In the

House and Senate!

Treason: *"Betrayal of one's country to an enemy."*
   Webster's New World Dictionary

Unfortunately both Houses of Congress have had their share of volatile anti-American misfits!

Some of the illustrious Congressional elite had envisioned tyrants of the totalitarian left as poor misunderstood neurotics. Or perhaps they were to be viewed as no more than wayward juvenile delinquents.

Still others consider an appeasement-minded pro-Communist foreign policy and no win wars as in Korea and Vietnam to be in the national interest!

Why are known Communists who vow to destroy America allowed to run for public office?

Why are known Communists who vow to destroy America allowed to be members of Congress?

Why is a Communist allowed to take the oath for the House or the Senate and swear to *"support and defend the Constitution of the United States against all enemies, foreign and domestic"* when, in fact, they are the enemy?

The oath of office for a Senator ends with *"So help you (Representative—'me') God."*

What meaning can this possibly have to a Communist who is by his very conditioning a professed atheist?

Yet, out and out Communist Party members have held and some still do hold seats in today's Congress!

One example was Augustus Freeman Hawkins who served in the House of Representatives from 1963 to 1991.

He was identified as a Red by John L. Leech, former organizer and State Committee member of the California Communist Party!

Another is Representative Charles Hayes who served in House from 1983 to 1993.

He was named by two witnesses during the 1950s as a Party member!

This Red was formerly vice-president of the United Food and Commercial Workers Union.

No one knows how many more there may be!

Yes some members of Congress have been and are a part of the international Communist conspiracy!

This is an unpleasant but undeniable fact!

A number of Representatives and Senators through ideology, blackmail, or sheer opportunism have allowed their names and position to be used to aid Communism through front organizations and subversive activities.

Adam Clayton Powell was a Congressman from Harlem in New York City. He served for 12 terms ranging from January 3, 1945-February 28, 1967.

Powell was affiliated with over 100 Communist Fronts.

He was also the featured speaker at many Communist Party fund raising gatherings!

Bella S. Abzug served in the House of Representatives from January 3, 1971-January 3, 1977.

She was director of the New York branch of the Communist National Lawyers Guild.

Abzug was also affiliated with a multitude of other Communist Fronts.

She helped found the International Association of Democratic Lawyers which is directly under the control of the KGB and the Central Committee of the Communist Party in Moscow!

Emanuel Cellar served 25 successive terms in Congress for almost 50 years. He was in office from March 1923 to January 1973.

This was despite his nearly 40 Communist Front affiliations and ventures!

The NLG was cited as never having *"failed to rally to the legal defense of the Communist Party and individual members thereof, including known espionage agents."*

Some House members boldly allowed Communist revolutionaries to use their office space.

The Red conspirators then organize activities against the best interests of the United States!

The distinguished historian Otto Scott revealed: *"There are men in Congress whose staffs are in constant touch with the Soviet Embassy; there are others in Congress whose careers have been based upon close associations with Communists and Communist causes.*

"For the first time in our history we see an American Congress that regards an American President as a worse enemy than an implacable foreign power that is already unloading troops and weapons on our own continent and that openly declares it seeks our defeat."

Read that again! It's unbelievable, but true!: ***"For the first time in our history we see an American Congress that regards an American President as a worse enemy than*** *an implacable foreign power that is already unloading troops and weapons on our own continent and that openly declares it seeks our defeat."*

Few Communists in the United States have so openly served the cause of the Red conspiracy as has Ronald Dellums. He was a Representative from California from 1971 until his resignation on February 6, 1998.

Following that he was a lobbyist until his election as the 47th mayor of Oakland.

Dellums was the first black elected to Congress from Northern California and the first openly socialist Congressman since World War II.

He let revolutionaries use his office space for planning the Communist May Day demonstrations in Washington!

Dellums provided committee Rooms to *"Hanoi"* Jane Fonda and radical leftist Tom Hayden in which to hold hate-filled anti-U.S. seminars.

He calls himself a Marxist!

Dellums sponsored, endorsed or cooperated with every major pro-Hanoi anti-American organization during the Vietnam War!

This leftist even pushed legislation to give special veteran's benefits. But these benefits were *only for* Americans who fought *for the Communists* during the Spanish Civil War!

Representative John Conyers was a member of the House representing Michigan's 14th congressional district which included parts of Detroit and Dearborn. A Democrat he started serving in 1965.

In January 2007, Conyers became chairman of the House Judiciary Committee.

He served on the Executive Board of the National Lawyers Guild.

This was no more than America's Moscow run Communist front for attorneys!

And he was featured with fugitive Weatherman member Bernardine Dohrn at the NLG's 31st annual meeting.

Bernardine Dohrn with her husband and fellow revolutionary Bill Ayers.

Ayers later engineered the illegal Presidential campaign of the infamous Barack Obama. This radical leftist has belonged to or associated with innumerable Communist Fronts!

He also participated in Red activities with Communist Party official Angela Davis and Communist attorney Mark Lane!

George W. Crockett was yet another Congressional member of the Communist National Lawyers Guild.

He'd been intimately associated with the Communist Party, Communists, Communist Front organizations and Communist causes for some 40 years!

This radical leftist attorney served in the House of Representatives from 1980 to 1991.

Crockett defended 11 Communist Party leaders who were tried and convicted under the *Smith Act*.

So outrageous was Crockett's courtroom behavior that Judge Harold Medina sentenced him to four months in jail for contempt!

He died at the age of 88 in 1997.

Senator Howard Morton Metzenbaum served for almost 20 years as a Democratic member of the U.S. Senate from Ohio (1974, 1976–1995).

He was once an official in the National Lawyers Guild and was formerly associated with quite a number of other subversive Front groups.

This outrageous leftist showed a devotion to Communist causes over the years.

Senator Claude D. *"Red"* Pepper was a close friend of two well known subversives -- Eleanor and Franklin Roosevelt.

This should tell us something!

Investigative journalist John Rees reported that Pepper *"carried the torch for Stalin in the U.S. Senate and amassed a never equaled record as the most openly pro-Communist member in the history of that august body."*

Senator Alan Cranston served in the Senate from 1969 to 1993.

Cranston began his career as a protégé of Communist spy Louis Adamic.

He knowingly hired Communist Party organizer David Karr (formerly Katz) and other Reds while working for the heavily infiltrated Office of War Information.

Cranston was denied a security clearance by Army Intelligence in July of 1944 yet he edited *Army Talk* while working for Communist Major Julius Schreiber.

The propaganda Cranston wrote for the consumption of American troops was so blatant that it was reprinted by the *Daily Worker*!

Cranston's entire adult life has been one of close association with Communists and Communist goals.

Senator Edmund Muskie (CFR) served as Governor of Maine, as U.S. Senator, as U.S. Secretary of State and ran as a candidate for President of the United States.

This leftist audaciously defended the Communist-led pro-Hanoi demonstrators who defiantly waved Vietcong flags.

In March 1970 he said: *"These people are not traitors!*

"They are patriots!"

Ignoring the thousands of young Americans who had been butchered in Vietnam he coldly commented that a Communist takeover *"doesn't bother me."*

Muskie was appropriately rewarded by President Jimmy Carter when he replaced another radical leftist Cyrus Vance (CFR) as Secretary of State.

Maurice Robert *"Mike"* Gravel is a former Democratic United States Senator from Alaska who served two terms from 1969 to 1981.

This rabid leftist gained a well-deserved reputation as being politically to the left of Karl Marx!

Gravel once sponsored a showing of *Brazil: A Report on Torture* in the Senate Office Building auditorium.

This was no more than a propaganda film of the most blatant kind!

The purported documentary attacked the anti- Communist pro-U.S. Brazilian Government.

The movie was actually shot in Chile not Brazil!

Propaganda printed by the SDS was distributed to the viewers.

Here a United States Senator knowingly sponsored a Communist propaganda movie.

The film stars terrorists trained in Communist Occupied Cuba.

It was produced by Reds in Communist Occupied Chile.

And the showing was accompanied by Communist literature handed out by Communist revolutionaries!

Was Comrade Gravel a Communist?

He's never been officially identified as one!

But the words of Confucius strike home in this case: *"Look at the means a man employs; consider his motives; observe his pleasures. A man simply cannot conceal himself."*

And once again consider the words of Joseph Stalin who was the worst mass murderer in history: *"Some are members of the Party, and some are not; but that is a formal difference.*

"The important thing is that both serve the same common purpose."

Who would have believed the Soviet KGB and their Communist Bloc counterparts would be able to place spies in at least nine Congressional offices?

And that Communist espionage agents operated on a number of Congressional committee staffs?

Or that a leftist Senator Christopher J. Dodd (CFR) would share jet-setter Bianca Jagger's sexual favors with Tomas Borge the animalistic mass-murdering butcher who ran Communist Occupied Nicaragua's secret police organization?

Dodd served in the House of Representatives from Connecticut from 1975 until 1981 when he became a Senator.

He served as general chairman of the Democratic National Committee from 1995 to 1997.

Or that 10 radical members of the House would arrogantly sign the traitorous *"Dear Commadante"* letter in support of Nicaragua's Communist dictator Daniel Ortega?

Who would have dreamed that many members of Congress were on Soviet espionage agent Orlando Letelier's *"contact list"*?

That at least two United States Senators would have taken money from Letelier who was known to be a dangerous KGB man?

One was leftist James George Abourezk who represented South Dakota from 1973 until 1979.

He was the first Arab-American to serve in the United States Senate.

The other was avid socialist Michael Harrington.

And who would have dreamed that 249 members of the House would vote against giving the Judiciary Committee $300,000 to investigate Communist activities in the United States?

Why?

Perhaps they feared exposure as moles on the payroll of their Kremlin masters.

These are but a few of the traitorous shenanigans openly taking place in America!

Security risks, Communist agents, terrorists and those who actively aid and abet them operate confidently throughout government and society.

There's little fear of exposure!

There's even less fear of prosecution!

All of this is the direct result of America having been quietly stripped of any internal security apparatus.

There is no official or congressional committee left that is willing to investigate, spotlight and punish the brazen acts of treason taking place daily in and out of government!

Epilogue

The record covering crucial episodes of the McCarthy era has been massively and deliberately distorted from the very beginning!

Conveniently forgotten or deliberately overlooked are the 78 hearings held between 1951 and 1952 by Senator William E. Jenner's (R-Indiana) Senate Internal Security Subcommittee (SISS); the House Committee On Internal Security; the House Un-American Activities Committee (HUAC) under the chairmanship of both Martin Dies (D-Texas) and Francis Walters (D-Pa); the Federal Bureau of Investigation (FBI) under the guidance of J. Edgar Hoover; and other investigating committees and individuals.

Out of all of these investigations one man was selected:

To be stopped!
To be destroyed!
To be made an example!

Why?

So that no one would ever again dare to initiate any investigations into the penetration of our government agencies by communist agents (spies) in the employ of the Soviet Union!

Yes!

An obscure Senator from Wisconsin was deliberately targeted for this purpose!

Joseph McCarthy's incredibly successful investigations panicked those on the political left.

Their reaction was shockingly quick!

Key data was been suppressed, denied and even widely falsified.

This took place in the media, all branches of government and many alleged scholars entrenched in the ivory towers of our institutions of higher learning!

Such misreporting and misrepresentation of the facts continues today.

Much of the misinformation we were (and still are today) so carefully spoon-fed about Senator Joseph McCarthy the man and his investigations was no more than an admixture of uncheckable blovations from deceased third parties and demonstratable falsehoods!

For example, how many innocent people were harmed by McCarthy's revelations?

The correct answer?

Not one!

No!

Not One!

McCarthy's most virulent critics have had more than a half century to produce the names of the hundreds of innocent people they claim were destroyed by the astounding revelations of the Senator from Wisconsin.

Yet those highly skilled propagandists in our media and government and institutions of higher learning have been unable to name even one innocent person they claim was destroyed after being falsely accused by McCarthy!

How many innocent people committed suicide as a result of McCarthy's exposure?

The correct answer?

Not one!

Not one suicide can be attributed to the investigations conducted by McCarthy!

No! Not one!

According to the obscene claims made the highly skilled propagandists in our media, government and scholars entranced in those ivory towers of our colleges and universities there were a rash of suicides with bodies falling constantly of the heads of pedestrians below on the streets of Manhattan!

Once again, McCarthy's most virulent critics have had more than 50 years to produce the names of the hundreds of innocent people they claim committed suicide because of the astounding revelations of the Senator from Wisconsin.

Yet those highly skilled propagandists in our media and government and institutions of higher learning have been unable to name even one innocent person they claim committed suicide after being falsely accused by McCarthy!

No!

Not one!

But there were two suicides on record during the McCarthy period!

Neither was the result of an innocent person who'd been ruined by McCarthy's revelations!

Both were subversives who'd been exposed by McCarthy!

Both were subversives who'd been positively indentified as Kremlin agents!

Lawrence Duggan had been operating in the State Department as a widely known Soviet spy!

He'd been called to testify before a Congressional investigating committee.

Duggan never made it!

He conveniently "fell" from a window high up in a Manhattan skyscraper!

Fell?

Probably not!

He was more than likely pushed from or tossed out of the window by an assassin in the employ of the Soviet Union!

Why?

To make certain he didn't fold under pressure and start naming other Kremlin moles.

Secondly there was the unexpected demise of Harry Dexter White.

This Soviet agent discovered that he was being investigated by J. Edgar Hoover of the FBI!

He died of a sudden heart attack!

Coincidence?

Not hardly!

Was White's death a suicide?

Yes or at least so claimed McCarthy's critics!

Again, not hardly!

Heart attacks can readily be induced with the proper use of certain medicines administered by a hired assassin in the employ of the Kremlin!

Why?

Simply to eliminate anyone who might panic and decide to turncoat and reveal the names of other spies secretly entrenched deeply in the bowels of every branch of our government.

To sum up, most fit into one of three categories:

Conscience lacking incurable liars!

Those with an axe to grind!

Individuals who simply do not know the facts!

If you liked this book in the *None Dare Call It Treason* series then you'll probably also enjoy reading the others!

Gift copies of this book can be ordered at

createspace.com/4213508

Available Titles

None Dare Call It Treason Book 1
The Internal Security Farce!
5.5" x 8.5" 97 pages $4.95
Order from createspace.com/4215951

None Dare Call It Treason Book 2
Never Ending Subversion
In Government!
5.5" x 8.5" 202 pages $4.95
Order from createspace.com/4216115

None Dare Call It Treason Book 3
America's Subversive State Department
Bloated With Security Risks
5.5" x 8.5" 202 pages $4.95
Order from createspace.com/4216626

None Dare Call It Treason Book 4
America's Illustrious State Department!
It's Machiavellian Misdeeds!
5.5" x 8.5" 202 pages $4.95
Order from createspace.com/4215018

None Dare Call It Treason Book 5
Our Presidents A Major Security Threat!
5.5" x 8.5" 202 pages $4.95
Order from createspace.com/4213501

None Dare Call It Treason Book 6
Presidential Words & Deeds
&Blatant Lies!
5.5" x 8.5" 202 pages $4.95
Order from createspace.com/4213920

None Dare Call It Treason Book 7
Subversives Close To Our Presidents
5.5" x 8.5" 89 pages $4.95
Order from createspace.com/4213931

None Dare Call It Treason Book 8
Henry Kissinger
The Shadowy Untouchable Kremlin Spy!
5.5" x 8.5" 202 pages $4.95
Order from createspace.com/4214986

None Dare Call It Treason Book 9
Inexcusably Arming America's Enemies!
5.5" x 8.5" 202 pages $4.95
Order from createspace.com/4216634

None Dare Call It Treason Book 10
Inexcusably Financing
America's Enemies!
5.5" x 8.5" 202 pages $4.95
Order from createspace.com/4216777

None Dare Call It Treason Book 11
Treasonous   Trade With & Aid To
Enemies Of Freedom!
5.5" x 8.5" 202 pages $4.95
Order from createspace.com/4216873

None Dare Call It Treason Book 12
*Wholesale Treason During the War
In Vietnam!*
5.5" x 8.5" 202 pages $4.95
Order from createspace.com/4215293

None Dare Call It Treason Book 13
*Big Business
& Astounding Acts Of Treason!*
5.5" x 8.5" 202 pages $4.95
Order from createspace.com/4215805

None Dare Call It Treason Book 14
*Illegally Importing
Slave Made Goodies!*
5.5" x 8.5" 202 pages $4.95
Order from createspace.com/4215894

None Dare Call It Treason Book 15
*The House That Hiss Built
The Anti-American United Nations!*
5.5" x 8.5" 202 pages $4.95
Order from createspace.com/4215323

None Dare Call It Treason Book 16
Security Risks in the House and Senate!
5.5" x 8.5" 202 pages $4.95
Order from createspace.com/4213508

None Dare Call It Treason Book 17
The Supreme Court A Devastating
Threat To National Security!
5.5" x 8.5" 202 pages $4.95
Order from createspace.com/4213699

Orders for Resale
40% Off Retail Price

Send Purchase Order to

christianamerica2@yahoo.com

MEET THE

AUTHOR

Robert W. Pelton has been writing and lecturing for more than 45 years on political, religious and historical subjects.

He has published more than 100 books including the sensational exposé *Unwanted Dead or Alive – The Greatest Act of Treason in Our History – The betrayal of American POWs Following World War II, Korea and Vietnam.*

Robert W. Pelton proudly claims a heritage going all the way back to well before the War for American Independence.

One of Mr. Pelton's ancestors, John Rogers, came to America on the Mayflower and was one of 41 signers of the Mayflower Compact.

Another, John Smith was one of the founders of Jamestown.

Peleg Pelton served as the fifer in the Continental Army at age 18 during the Battle of Saratoga (1777) and again in Yorktown (1781).

Captain Peter Hager was Commander of the Old Stone Fort in Schoharie, New York, in 1780.

Another, Captain Bezaleel Tyler fought in the only Revolutionary War Battle taking place in Sullivan County, New York.

Mr. Pelton is a member of Sons of the Revolution (SOR), and Sons of the American Revolution (SAR).

* 9 7 8 1 4 8 3 9 0 8 5 9 5 *